D1320928

GOD'S MADCAP

Amy and the Children

GOD'S MADCAP

The Story of Amy Carmichael of Dohnavur

by
NANCY E. ROBBINS
Dohnavur Fellowship

LUTTERWORTH PRESS
LONDON

First published 1962
Second impression 1963
Third impression 1964
Fourth impression 1968

COPYRIGHT © NANCY E. ROBBINS 1962

7188 0874.6

PRINTED IN GREAT BRITAIN PHOTOLITHO
BY EBENEZER BAYLIS AND SON, LTD.
THE TRINITY PRESS, WORCESTER, AND LONDON

CONTENTS

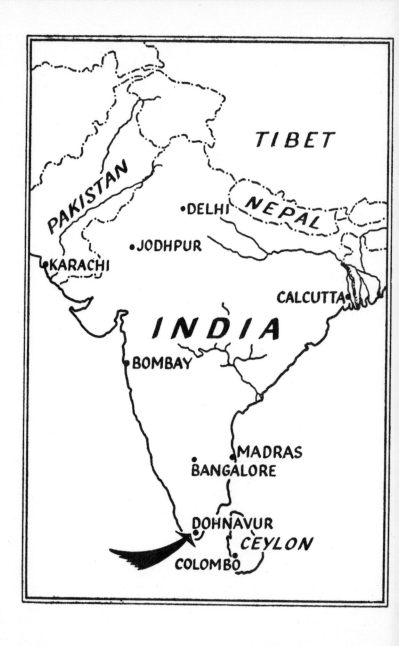

1

TWO TEA-PARTIES, AND SOME ADVENTURES

LATE in the afternoon of December 16, 1950, crowds of people, big and little, old and young, were walking sedately as befitted their years, or running and skipping excitedly as was suitable to the occasion, towards the tree-fringed field under the big clock tower at Dohnavur in South India. Everyone seemed to be talking at once, and it did not matter a bit that no one was paying any attention to what anyone else was saying.

There on the grass, arranged in several big circles, were lots and lots of dark green shiny plantain leaves. On each leaf was a tempting array of Indian delicacies. There were fluffy white rice-cakes with tasty orange-coloured chutney, and crisp fried sweet-meats, and curly crunchy *murukku* and fat yellow bananas, and beside each leaf a brass tumbler glinting in the sunshine all ready for the hot sweet coffee shortly to be poured into it.

The people quickly took their places before the

leaves prepared for them. The afternoon sun shone warmly on the gay blues and reds, yellows and mauves of their clothes and lent brilliance to the scene. At first everyone stood waiting. Soon the whistle would blow and then grace would be said and they would all sit down and begin to enjoy this wonderful feast. In the meanwhile many of the smaller children, impatient of formalities, bent intently over their leaves to examine the contents. Small fingers probed inquiringly and surreptitious licks seemed to yield satisfactory results. The feast was up to expected standards.

What was it all about?

Anyone presuming to ask any of the children such an ignorant question would have been met by an astonished look. "Why, don't you know?" the child would have said. "Today is our Amma's (mother's) birthday."

Amy Carmichael, mother of this Family of about nine hundred people who were about to sit down to a birthday feast in her honour, was not out there in the sunshine with them. She was lying ill, in her room not very far away. She was old now, and tired too, but she loved to think of her children's happiness on this bright afternoon. How vividly she could picture them all! Her room was full of flowers, and the table by her bed and all other available spaces were covered with cards and letters and little gifts, tokens of her family's love and thought for her on this special day. If she turned her head just a little, she could see a polished board hanging on the wall on which were painted the words "Good . . . Acceptable . . . Perfect". Yes, that was right. God's will for every part of her long life had been just that, and even to the end it would be so.

On that last birthday afternoon, did her mind travel back over the years to the beginning of the story? Did she, perhaps, see herself at another very different tea-party?

*   *   *

It was a miserable day. Cold gusts of wind blew down the Belfast streets and seemed to penetrate even the warmest coats and wraps. The rain beat dismally on to the roads and roof-tops and splashed up round the ankles of anyone brave enough to venture out. Passing horse-carts spattered the pavements with mud. The sky was leaden and it looked as if the sun would never shine again.

Amy Carmichael was not thinking about the weather. For her every prospect was rosy. She and her mother were having a tea-party, just the two of them, in a tea-shop. She had never seen such a dazzling array of different cakes and good things to eat. Making a choice was a serious business.

9

While she was deeply absorbed in this delectable occupation, she suddenly noticed a little face pressed against the window of the café, watching her. She wished the owner of the face would go away. She hated being observed so intently, and somehow did not enjoy her tea very much after all. Eventually it was time to go. Her mother paid the waitress, and together they left the tea-shop. Now at last Amy was able to have a good look at the owner of the hungry eyes who had watched her so closely all through tea-time. She was a poor little girl. In spite of the bitter day, she had no coat, only a ragged cotton frock that clung wetly to her in the wind. She had no shoes and her feet were quite blue with cold. She just could not take her longing eyes off the tempting display of cakes in the shop window. She looked dreadfully thin, and obviously had not had any tea. Amy wondered unhappily whether she had had any breakfast or lunch either.

Amy was very quiet on the way home. It was nice to get indoors out of the rain, and she sat in front of a big fire toasting her toes thoughtfully. At last she got up and searched for a pencil. Then writing laboriously with large letters in an old scrap-book, she solemnly recorded her secret resolve:

When I grow up and money have
I know what I will do,
I'll build a great big lovely place
For little girls like you.

Then she forgot all about it.

*　　*　　*

There were so many interesting things to do at her home in Millisle, in Northern Ireland. The grey stone house stood in a lovely big garden where Amy and her brothers and sisters could play thrilling games. Or they could go and explore the beach, daring each other to brave the big breakers and flying spray, and stand on the slippery sea-wall at high tide. At home there was a dear marmalade cat, and a faithful collie who could be counted upon to share their escapades. Amy also had a frisky pony called Fanny whose high spirits matched her own. Her father taught her to ride. He said that she must always be patient, and never nag. He taught her to ride with a very light rein. He never had to encourage her not to be afraid, she was absolutely fearless, and there was nothing she loved better than to race at top speed along the sea-shore on Fanny's back.

There generally seemed to be a quite new, or fairly new, baby at home, too, for Amy was the eldest of a family of seven. She liked playing with the babies and admiring their tiny pink toes and the way they clutched her fingers with their little tight fists. As they grew older she taught them to be loyal accomplices in her madcap plans and adventures.

When she was very small Amy was given a beautiful dolls' house furnished in fine style for smartly dressed dolls. She thought the dolls very dull, and swept out the furniture which seemed to her both ordinary and uninteresting. She then lovingly prepared a home for more congenial occupants. She filled the rooms with soft green moss and lovely coloured stones. Then she brought in active beetles and lively earwigs to live there. Unfortunately the grown-ups did not share her love for creepy-crawlies, and her beloved beetles were turned out into the garden again. On another occasion she found a poor mouse drowning in a bucket of water. She rescued it and was just trying to get it dry and comfortable again, when the bell rang for family prayers. It would never do to be late, so she trotted off with the mouse under her pinafore. She did hope that no one would notice. Grown-up people were sometimes quite queer about dear little mice. Her father began reading the lesson in his deep quiet voice, and everyone sat listening in reverent silence. Suddenly there was a loud high squeak, a quite unsuitable comment on the reading, and it seemed to come from Amy's place!

Mr. and Mrs. Carmichael always took their family to church on Sundays. The children used to pick themselves small nosegays of favourite flowers before setting out, so as to have something pretty to look at during the sermon, which was always very long. Picture books were *never* allowed in church, but peppermints could be sucked, and these were a great consolation. Amy certainly found church a trial, and even her fertile imagination was hard put to it to find ways of whiling away the time she was expected to sit quiet and still in her pew. She was still very young, however, when she first began to notice that her mother's prayers really did something. God heard them, and He answered them too, there was no doubt about that.

She decided to try an experiment in prayer on her own. Her mother, whom she greatly admired, had bright blue eyes. Amy's own eyes were brown which she considered very inferior. So one night, full of hope, she knelt and asked God to change her eyes and make them blue instead of brown. Early in the morning, her heart pounding away with excitement, she pushed a chair over to the dressing-table and clambered up to examine her new blue eyes in the mirror. She nearly fell off the chair with disappointment and surprise. Her eyes were still as brown as brown. God had not answered her prayer. It was no good, she would never pray again. Even as she made this bitter resolve, she seemed to hear a quiet voice saying somewhere "God said 'no'. Isn't 'no' an answer?" She had to admit that "no" can be an answer, and decided that perhaps it would be silly to stop praying just because God had said "no" once.

Some time after this on a day when their father and mother had gone out, Amy and two of her brothers saw a golden opportunity to fulfil a long-cherished ambition. They ran to the bathroom at the top of the tall old house and succeeded with difficulty in opening the skylight over the bath. They then scrambled up and wriggled and squeezed themselves out on to the roof. It was hard work and Amy had to encourage her two little brothers to prevent them from giving up and going back. How good it was when they emerged hot and breathless into the clean cold breeze on the roof-top. They could look down on the tops of the smaller trees and admire the gaily-coloured patterns made by the flower beds far below. Amy had not come up through that difficult skylight just for sightseeing, however; she intended to walk right round the house on the gutter. She set out on this perilous journey in triumphant high spirits with her two younger brothers gamely following. All went well until they had rounded a difficult corner and then, horror of all horrors, who should they see looking up at them from the front garden but their father and mother. Mr. Carmichael could be rather stern on occasions, and this was such an occasion. The journey was cut short, and the glorious adventure ended painfully for poor Amy.

*　　*　　*

When Amy grew older, her parents decided to send her to a boarding school in England. To her the school seemed like a drab colourless prison. Life had been such fun and so free and adventurous with her brothers in Ireland. Now she was cramped and frustrated by lots of rules and regulations. At first the other girls did not know what to make of the wild Irish rebel who had arrived in their midst and who was so often in trouble with the authorities, but soon she became popular. In spite of this, poor Amy was very homesick. Her high spirits and bright ideas so often ended in disgrace and punishment, when she had really intended no harm at all. In time she settled down a bit and became very fond of some of the staff, and made some good friends among the girls too, but in her opinion nothing very interesting or exciting ever happened at school.

There was just one notable exception to this rule. Towards the end of her school days a member of the staff of the Children's Special Service Mission, Mr. Edwin Arrowsmith, came to Harrogate to hold a mission. His talks were very different from the long sermons that she had often endured, and somehow reminded her of the way her mother used to talk. His prayers too were like her mother's, just friendly talks with a well-loved Person. The stories he told fired her imagination and enthralled her, but that was not all. Afterwards she could never say exactly how it happened, but on one memorable day during a few moments' quiet at the end of a meeting, she knew that she had met with the living Lord Jesus and that He had become her very own Saviour and Shepherd. This was quite the biggest and most wonderful thing that had ever happened to her.

2

AMY MEETS THE SHAWLIES

SHORTLY after Amy left her English boarding school, the Carmichael family sold up their house in Millisle, and moved to Belfast. Then quite suddenly an unexpected blow fell upon the family. Mr. Carmichael became ill, and almost before his children had realized that the illness was in any way dangerous, he died. All the children except Amy were still at school, and she suddenly found herself faced with the big responsibility of helping her mother and brothers and sisters in this new and difficult situation. They were poorer than they had ever been before—and were to become poorer yet—but Amy was always a tower of strength to them all, and full of practical suggestions of ways and means of managing happily on a little. Her two younger sisters were often prevented by illness from attending school regularly, so Amy taught them at home. She was a lively and original teacher, and lessons with her were great fun.

In spite of all this, there was not sufficient out-let at home for all Amy's overflowing energy.

Besides, something very tremendous had happened to her back at Harrogate, and every day since that special day she had come to know the Lord Jesus a little better. He was her Friend. He had given her courage when her father died so suddenly, and even when family affairs could have seemed very perplexing and worrying. He had given her peace too. She found herself just longing to tell other people of the joy that she had found. She saw so many sad people in Belfast, people whose lives seemed filled with nothing but sorrow and poverty and dull hopelessness.

There were the children in the streets behind her home, for instance. They had nowhere to play except the dirty muddy gutters. They always looked hungry and thin, and their clothes were ragged and drab. They quarrelled and shouted at each other, and now and then were scolded or beaten by their loud-voiced hard-worked mothers. Amy's heart went out to them. She went around and invited them to come to a children's meeting in her home on Sunday afternoons. They followed her as though she were the Pied Piper. She made them so welcome, and told them such stories, and the room where they met was so clean and bright and warm, and Mrs. Carmichael always had something so good for them to eat before they went home, that it was no wonder they loved to attend that meeting. Amy had a practical colleague in her mother and one who was not afraid of doing unusual things, even if her fashionable friends did raise their eyebrows and shake their heads at her.

*　　*　　*

Somebody introduced Amy to Mr. Montgomery, a leader in the Belfast City Mission. On Saturday evenings he used to take her round some of the poorer districts of the city. She noticed the mill-girls drifting about the streets aimlessly in the shawls that earned them the nickname of "Shawlies". They worked long hours in the mills all the week, but their wages were not big enough to allow them to indulge in even the cheapest of hats, and in those far-off days a hat was a *must* for any girl or woman who wanted to be the least bit smart. They seemed to have absolutely nothing to make life worth living. Amy was so happy herself, she longed to be able to share some of her happiness with these unfortunate girls, many of whom were about her own age. She wondered if they knew anything about the love of the Lord Jesus. None of them went to church as far as she knew; the suggestion seemed absurd to the girls. "Go to church? Who, me? And what'd the smart toffs say if they found a 'Shawlie' in their seat?" Amy had no difficulty in thinking what the fashionable ladies *would* say, but she thought of another plan.

She went to see a Presbyterian minister whom she knew and asked him for permission to run a meeting for "Shawlies" only, on Sunday mornings in his church hall. He looked at her thoughtfully, she was such a small slip of a girl. "Do you think you will be able to do it?" he asked. "It is easier to start a thing like that than to keep it up, you know." Amy had not much confidence in her own abilities, but she believed that this was a job that she could do, first of all because God had put the thought into her head, and secondly because the more she thought of the mill-girls the more she found herself loving them. Love makes all sorts of hard things easy. The minister was satisfied, but some of his congregation were not.

"That young Amy Carmichael doesn't know what she is undertaking," they said. "Those rough, bad-mannered, dirty girls will just run riot. What would they want to come to church for? Hymns and sermons are not in their line. Very likely they will break the place up; and think of the things Amy may catch from them!"

Fortunately for Amy her mother was on her side, and was not put off even when the minister's wife herself said darkly, "I would let no child of mine go down those streets."

The Sunday meeting was a success from the very beginning. Amy was an enthusiast, and her enthusiasm soon fired others, and a band of helpers joined her in her work. Some of these people were older than Amy, who was still in her teens, but she was always the leader.

3

"ASK NO ONE BUT GOD?"

THE "Shawlies" attended the Sunday morning service in such numbers that quite soon the church hall was too small to accommodate all who wanted to come. Amy was now in a quandary, because if the work was to continue and grow, a new hall was an absolute necessity. She and her helpers talked and prayed over the matter.

"Have you seen this?" said one of them one day, holding up a Christian periodical. "This" proved to be an advertisement of an iron hall which could be erected for £500 and would hold five hundred people.

"Oh, look!" said another, looking longingly at the picture of the hall, as it would appear when completed; "it is just exactly what we need. But £500 is such a lot of money. How can we possibly raise it?"

"Should we ask the minister if we may make a special collection among the church members? Some of them are very rich, and could easily give quite a lot—if only they would."

Amy was thinking hard. When she was ten or

eleven, she had been asked to collect money for a home for poor children. One day she had taken her collecting-card to a rich man who was living in a big house that he had just built for himself. He had sent her off without giving a penny for the children, and this miserable experience had made a lasting impression on her mind. That man had not wanted to give, perhaps he did not even love the Lord Jesus.

"Do you think that God could make His own people *want* to give money for His work without being asked?" she said, rather shyly. This was rather a poser to the others, who, not having had the same experience, had not thought much about this matter. They supposed, somewhat doubtfully, that He could, but they wondered how the people would know that there was any need if someone did not tell them.

"God does know about our need of a hall, and we do believe that He has told us to hold this meeting for the girls. Do you think that we could agree together to pray for £500, and not ask anyone else but God Himself?" inquired Amy. "After all, if we begin to ask people, we can easily make mistakes, but God does not make mistakes. Don't you think it would really be safer just to pray?" Amy made her suggestion with some diffidence. She felt sure that God had given her these thoughts as she had read some of the Bible promises about prayer, but she had never heard of anyone who had prayed secretly for money and received it. However, eventually they all agreed to fall in with her proposal, and began to pray most earnestly for £500.

*　　*　　*

Amy and her friends had not been praying in this way for very long when Amy received an invitation to lunch with a lady whom she had never met before. The lady had heard from friends something about the meeting for mill-girls in the church hall, and she wanted to meet the leader and hear more from her about the girls. Amy never forgot the kindness of her hostess who questioned her so eagerly about the "Shawlies", their meeting and their needs. A day or two later she received a letter from her saying that she would like to give £500 towards buying and erecting a new hall for them.

There was still the problem of obtaining a building site. Land was very expensive in Belfast. Someone suggested that perhaps a certain mill-owner would lease land to them near the mills that belonged to him. The thought of going to see this important business man and explaining to him what she wanted really horrified Amy. Perhaps he would be angry, or perhaps he would just laugh at her and the whole project, and send her about her business. She did not like it, but felt it was worth risking making a fool of herself for God's sake and for the sake of the mill-girls. So in fear and trembling, and yet full of hope, she went alone to face the great man.

He was kinder than she had thought likely even in her wildest dreams. He willingly granted the lease of a suitable piece of land. When she asked about the rent and heard the answer, she could hardly believe her ears. He asked a purely nominal sum, just as a formality. The land was virtually a gift.

Experiment had proved that the Bible is right, God does answer prayer, and He often gives much bigger and better things than we would have thought of asking for ourselves. What a good thing Amy did not stop praying when she had "no" for an answer, when she was a little girl.

After this the work went ahead by leaps and bounds. The girls wanted to meet on week-days as well as on Sundays. Soon Amy had clubs and meetings arranged for them on almost every evening of the week in the new hall, which was called the Welcome. She continued to ask only God for the money she needed for the work, and she found it a very safe and practical way of doing things.

One day some poor girls came in who were badly in need of a meal. Amy had nothing to give them, and no money with which to buy anything. She and the girls knelt and told God of the need. Even as they prayed, a man walked quietly into the hall, dropped half a sovereign on to a table, and walked quietly out again. In those days 10s. would buy quite a lot, and it seemed to Amy almost as though the money had dropped straight from Heaven.

* * *

The years passed quickly and the circumstances of the Carmichael family changed. The two older boys emigrated to America. Some time later the younger boys also left Belfast, one to settle in Canada and the other in South Africa.

When Amy was twenty-one, an old friend of the family asked her to go to Ancoats, Manchester, to work among factory girls there. At the same time her mother was offered a congenial post in the same town. The boys no longer needed them in Belfast, and it seemed right for Amy and one of her sisters to go with Mrs. Carmichael to Manchester. The lady who had given the money to build the Welcome was able and willing to take over the leadership of the work there, which has continued to flourish, though on somewhat different lines, until today.

It did not take Amy long to become absorbed in the new job, and she threw herself into it with whole-hearted enjoyment and soon became extremely busy. She seldom had time to cook proper meals for herself, and she was short of sleep too. At last her health gave way, and she was very reluctantly compelled to give up her slum work and take a rest.

Another friend of the Carmichael family, Mr. Robert Wilson, invited Amy to stay at his lovely home in the Lake District. His wife had recently died, and so had his only daughter, a girl of about Amy's age, so he was very lonely. He soon became greatly attached to Amy, and eventually asked her mother if she could spare her for the greater part of the year to take the place of his own daughter. To this Mrs. Carmichael unselfishly agreed, and Amy settled to a pleasant if less eventful kind of life.

4

IN SUNRISE LAND

IT WAS a far cry from the back streets of Belfast and the vermin-infested slums of Manchester to the spacious comfort of Broughton Grange, and the green lanes and wooded hills of the Lake District. Mr. Wilson soon found out about Amy's love of animals. He gave her a pony on which she explored the countryside, and a black-and-tan terrier called Scamp, who became her inseparable friend. How she revelled in the beauty all around her.

Mr. Wilson was one of the founders of the Keswick Convention, the great gathering of Christian people held every summer at Keswick, and he was a much sought-after speaker for conference meetings. He had a large correspondence. Amy helped him with his letters, and was his constant companion. She came to think of him as her "second father" and always called him the D.O.M. (which meant Dear Old Man). In addition to the help she gave him in all his work, she accepted responsibility both for a Scripture Union meeting for village children, and also for a girls'

Bible class. As well as this, she began to write articles for a Christian magazine.

It seemed to Amy that the D.O.M. needed her, and that it would be her job to stay and help him for the rest of his life. Then quite suddenly, on one snowy winter's evening, God spoke to her very clearly. He told her that He wanted her to serve Him overseas as a missionary. This was the most difficult thing Amy had ever been asked to do. She would have loved to go abroad to tell people about a God who loves them, but as she thought of the D.O.M. and her mother, and of how terribly they would miss her, she could hardly bear the thought of leaving them. How could she hurt them when they loved her so? Could God really want her to leave people who seemed to need her so badly? Amy spent the night battling the question out. In the morning she knew what she must do, and she wrote a letter to her mother, and then told the D.O.M., too, of God's word to her, and of her decision to obey.

The D.O.M. was shattered with grief at the prospect of losing his dear adopted daughter, but he could say nothing to hinder her from obeying a Voice which he, too, loved to obey. Mrs. Carmichael was sad at the thought of parting, but bravely and unhesitatingly encouraged her to do what she believed to be right.

As other people came to hear of this decision, a

positive storm of protest broke over Amy's head. Nearly everyone thought that she was making a dreadful and very selfish mistake. "Do you want to kill the D.O.M. after he has been so kind to you?" they asked. The whole situation was almost unbearably painful to her, and yet she felt sure that there could not be any lasting happiness for any of them if she disobeyed God and took what looked like the easy path of staying at home.

* * *

It was over a year before all obstacles were finally overcome and Amy boarded a ship for the first stage of her journey to Japan, where she was going to join Mr. and Mrs. Barclay Buxton, in their work at Matsuye.

The journey was long and uncomfortable. At length, after nearly two months of weary travelling and some lively adventures, she arrived at her destination and took up her new life and work.

Amy took an immediate liking to the Japanese people, whom she found friendly and charming. She admired their beautiful clothes, their taste in flower decoration, their pictures, and their lovely country. There was nothing ugly anywhere. Their politeness was quite staggering. Amy wondered if she would ever learn the proper way to bow, the right words of humility and contempt to use when speaking of herself, and the correct terms of admiration and respect with which to address everyone else. Then she had to learn to sit on the floor. There were no chairs or beds in most Japanese homes, and the floor gets quite hard after a while, specially if the conversation with which one is being regaled seems unintelligible gibberish! It was no use leaning wearily against a wall for support either, for they were all made of paper. Then there was the food—she quite often wrote home about this. If you had only chopsticks to do it with, how would *you* tackle rice; raw fish, sliced and adorned with brown sea-weed; pickled plums; a creature with eyes in a bowl of soup; a cup of black beans in liquid like senna tea? What would you do if you were kindly offered a live whelk impaled on a none-too-clean pin? Amy had to solve these problems and many more.

Quite a lot of Amy's time had to be spent in language study, but workers were few and there was much to be done, so she eagerly agreed to begin to teach in the villages right away. Of course this meant speaking through an interpreter, which is a very slow, tiring business, but Amy's enthusiasm carried her through all such difficulties quite undeterred, though she did long to be able to talk and understand without the help of a third person. She and Misaki San, the

Japanese lady with whom she worked, became fast friends.

They visited many villages, sometimes travelling long distances, and spending nights in wayside "hotels". Often they talked with people who had never before heard of the Lord Jesus. One day, as they wandered through a bamboo wood, villagers who lived in the houses half-hidden in the leafy tangle asked them to stop. "Have you ever heard of the one true God, who loves you?" asked Amy. "*One* God!" said the people, laughing as they pointed to a little open wayside shrine full of idols. "Why, look, there are many. Did you say He loves us? How amusing!" There was an old man among them, who had listened with amazement to the story of a God of love who died for our sins. He turned to the others and said slowly, "You are children, you have not heard much yet, but I am not a child and even I have *never* heard such honourable words."

Another day, towards sunset, they came upon three devout Buddhist men preparing for evening worship. One was arranging lilies before the family shrine. A lamp hung before an idol which was covered in chrysanthemums. Amy and her friend got into conversation with them, and soon they were listening to words from the Bible. The most thoughtful of the three men was tremendously impressed. "Buddha is dead," he said;

"he told us to be good, but he cannot give us the power to do it. If your teaching about a living God is true, you are an angel from heaven to us. But can you *show* us this life?" What a challenge! Amy never forgot that question. People do not want just words and teaching, they do want to see that the Lord Jesus really makes a difference to the things His followers say and do.

*   *   *

They did not always meet with such a friendly reception. There were those about who hated everything foreign, and who hated the Name of Christ above all things. On one occasion Buddhist agitators descended upon a Sunday service, tore the church doors off their hinges, stole everything they could lay hands on, and bombarded the place and the congregation with stones. The Christians tried to protect Amy, but as stones were coming from all directions there was not much that they could do.

Generally Amy's Japanese fellow-worker was willing to co-operate in all that Amy suggested doing; she too loved the Lord and wanted to serve Him to the very utmost. One day there was a hard thing to be done, and for once her courage failed her. "I don't want to do that," she said. Amy felt sure the thing in question must be done. How could she h lp her friend to want to do it? She remembered that one of her favourite hymns was "Onward, Christian soldiers", so she began to sing it for her encouragement—but she just changed the words a little as she went along:

"Onward, Christian soldiers,
    Sitting on the mats!
Nice and warm and cosy,
    Like little pussycats.
Onward, Christian soldiers,
    Oh how brave are we!
Don't we do our fighting
    Very comfortably?"

At first Amy's companion laughed at this ridiculous parody, but then she almost cried as she realized how wrong it is to sing hymns full of big, bold promises to God, and then to do something quite different. The hard job, needless to say, was done.

5

ANSWERED PRAYER

IN IRELAND and in England Amy had learnt quite a lot about the way God answers prayer. In Japan she learned a great deal more. Early one morning, word was brought to the house where she was living that a man in the next street was desperately ill. The people said that he was in the possession of the Fox demon. They worshipped this demon, and were very much afraid of him, because they believed that he did all sorts of frightful things to those who offended him in any way. As Amy listened to the rather fantastic story that was being told, she remembered that the Lord Jesus had said "All power is given unto Me . . . I am with you". She remembered how He had healed, and given power to His followers to heal too, at times. She wondered, did He want to bring glory to His own Name now by healing this poor man? Did He want her to do anything in the matter? The thought was terrifying. How awful it would be to make a mistake. She went to her own room and knelt down and asked God to show her what He wanted. It was long before she was quite certain of the answer. Eventually she went to her Japanese interpreter and asked her whether she believed that the Lord Jesus was willing to heal the man.

Misaki San was rather startled. It would be terrible to lose face by attempting something that did not work—far, far worse than making a fool of oneself in England, where people laugh and forget. In Japan it would be a lasting shame. Misaki San was a true disciple of the Lord, however, so she too prayed, and became convinced that the Lord *was* willing to heal this man. They sent a message round to his home asking whether they might be allowed to see him. In the meanwhile they continued to pray.

The answer came back that they might see him, but that he had "six foxes", was very wild and was tied up. They went to the house and were taken upstairs. Amy had prepared herself for something pretty bad, but this was worse than anything she had imagined. The man was lying on the floor strapped and tied to two crossbeams. His body was covered with sores and wounds. His friends had been trying to drive out the demons by putting little cones of powdered medicine on his skin and setting fire to them. The pain must have been terrible and he was wild and raving.

With confidence Amy told the man's wife and

his friends that the Lord Jesus was stronger than any demon, and that He could give healing. As soon as the Name of Jesus was spoken the man's violence became terrifying, and he shouted all sorts of blasphemy as he struggled and fought to get at Amy. She and Misaki San knelt to pray, but the poor demented man became worse and worse, and it was quite hopeless to try and stay in the room.

Amy felt desperate. What had she done wrong? She felt sure that God had told her to come, and His Name was being dishonoured in front of heathen people who would certainly not want to have anything more to do with Him. What *had* she done wrong? Even as she said good-bye, feeling absolutely desperate, she seemed to hear the words again, "All power is given unto Me . . . I AM WITH YOU." With new faith and courage, Amy said to the man's wife, "Our God will heal your husband. Let us know when the demon has left him. We will go home and pray until we hear from you."

Within an hour there was a message to say that the foxes had gone, the cords were off, the man was asleep. Next day he asked to see Amy and her companion, and listened gladly as they told him about the God who had healed him and who was now willing and able to forgive his sins and give him new life. He and his wife knelt together to pray to Him that night. He told all his friends what great things God had done for him, and continued to trust Him to the end of his life.

Buddhist priests who profess to be able to cast out demons always make a great parade of their own greatness, to impress their patient, and win his confidence. There had been nothing about Amy and her friend to impress, rather the reverse. All the honour of that cure went to God Himself —which was just what Amy had prayed.

*　　*　　*

Amy was only in Japan a little over a year, and then she became ill. It was a puzzling thing to her. She was ordered to spend a holiday in China, where the climate was thought to be more suitable for her kind of trouble. In Shanghai she became more ill than ever, and before long she found herself on her way to Ceylon, and eventually to England once more.

6

INDIA—NEW BEGINNINGS

THE Resident's carriage was coming up the long hill to the cantonments at a fine spanking pace, and there beside it, galloping for all she was worth on a rather small pony, was a young white woman. She was flushed and breathless but smiling and eager as she spurred her pony on to greater efforts. Would she make it? She put everything she had into the last lap, and just pulled ahead, dishevelled but triumphant.

Amy returned home in a tranquil frame of mind. It had been a lovely ride and to race like that had helped to get rid of the stuffiness and fustiness of a hard day of language study. What fun it had been!

Unfortunately, news of Amy's racing soon got about, and to her surprise she found herself in disgrace. She had apparently made an appalling exhibition of herself, and what's more, she had shown a shocking lack of respect for the Resident —the Queen's representative. In the end it almost sounded as if she had insulted Her Majesty herself!

Bangalore was very different from Japan, and Amy was not finding her first few months in India at all easy.

When she had arrived in England from Japan, she was not at all well. Various doctors saw her and told her that she would never be fit enough to work in the tropics again. Her friends all urged her to give up the idea of overseas service and to settle down at home. It was all very confusing but Amy was quite sure that God had called her for service abroad, and she could not believe that this service was already finished.

Then, quite out of the blue, came a letter from a friend who was working in Bangalore. The climate of Bangalore was very healthy, she said. More missionaries were needed there, why should not Amy come?

*   *   *

Amy acted on this suggestion, was accepted by the missionary society concerned, and in due course set out again on a long sea voyage, bound this time for India. At some stage in the journey to Bangalore, which was full of delays, she picked up one of the more unpleasant tropical fevers (sometimes called break-bone fever because of the horrible aches and pains which go with it), and arrived at her destination with a temperature of 105°. It was a long time before she felt really

well again, and this made a very depressing beginning for a new work.

As soon as she was fit, she began to study the
Urdu language. She had not got very far with
this, however, when she was asked to study Tamil
instead, as a Tamil-speaking evangelist was needed
for the hospital in the city. There are said to be
few languages more difficult to learn than Tamil,
and Amy grew discouraged over her slow progress.
The climate was not as pleasant as she had been
led to expect and there were lots of mosquitoes
and other tormenting insects, but worse than that,
she found it hard to get on with some of her
fellow-missionaries. One in particular seemed to
her to be unfair and dominating, and Amy had
to struggle with resentment and hurt pride when
she was sometimes ordered about and harshly
criticized. She was tempted to be very sorry for
herself as she looked back on the wonderful
experiences of the past, and compared them with
the drabness and petty annoyances of the present.
God had new lessons to teach her through these
new difficulties, however. She found that He was
able to deliver her from self-pity, that most time-
wasting occupation. She also found that He could
give her His love even for apparently unlovable
people. He is in fact a God who can change
dispositions.

After a while it was suggested that she would

learn better Tamil further south, where it is the only language spoken, than in Bangalore, where it is one of many languages. There was a missionary in the Tirunelveli District, Mr. Walker by name, who was a Tamil scholar of note, and he offered to coach her. She accepted his offer. Mr. Walker's clear, patient teaching was a great help and in due course, much to her surprise, Amy passed her language exams with flying colours.

Just at this time Mr. and Mrs. Walker were beginning village evangelistic work in an area new to them; a woman was needed to lead the women's work, and Amy stayed on to do this.

*   *   *

In some ways the work that she now began to do was similar to that which she had done in Japan. Her base was a village on the sandy plain with its numberless rustling palm trees. Among the trees were hundreds of other villages and to these Amy and her Indian fellow-workers went. Often they set out in the early morning, while it was still dark, in a springless bullock-cart, which jolted and rattled them over the deeply rutted roads at about three miles per hour. When they arrived at their destination they would walk through the streets, staying to talk to any who would listen to their message concerning the living God who loves us all.

It was not easy work. The people of India have ancient religions and a culture of their own which control their whole way of life. They are not anxious to change either the gods they worship or the way they live. The people of the area where Amy was were mostly very poor, and at that time hardly any of the girls or women were educated at all. Many of them had not seen a white woman before and were filled with horrified curiosity at the sight of Amy. One old lady to whom she tried to talk said that she had heard that white people were not really white all over, but were a kind of piebald. She asked Amy if she might examine her to get first-hand knowledge of this very strange phenomenon.

Another day as their bullock-cart approached a village, a child looked in to see who was coming. She rushed off shouting at the top of her voice, "Oh everyone come running and see! A great white man is here! Oh what an appalling spectacle! A great white man!"

Children appeared from everywhere all eyes and tongues.

"She isn't a man."

"He is!"

"She isn't!"

"He has got a man's turban!"

"But look at her *seelai*!"

Seelai is the Tamil word for the sari which is

43

the dress all Indian women wear and which Amy always wore too. She also wore a big hat to protect her from the hot sun. Indian men sometimes do this, but the women never do.

Well, at any rate Amy had no delusions about the way her appearance struck the village folk! When they had got over their surprise, they were often friendly and would receive her and her companions into their houses and sit and talk. Always there were a lot of questions first:

"Are you married or a widow?"

"What relations have you?"

"Where are they all?"

"Why have you left them all to come here?"

"What wages do you get for doing this work?"

These questions generally gave Amy an opening eventually to talk to the women about the Lord Jesus, for whose sake she had left her family. Sometimes they were not a bit interested. At other times one or more would seem to be listening with eyes fixed upon her. All too often it turned out that even their interest was really in something quite different. Leaning forward with an earnest expression as though about to ask an important and intelligent question on the subject of which Amy was speaking, a woman would ask, "How much did that *seelai* cost?", or, "What food do you eat? Do you eat curry and rice as we do?"

44

Amy appreciated the humour of all this, but her heart ached for these people whom she was beginning to love very much. Their religion tells of gods who are said to have come to this world to destroy evil, but in doing this they also destroyed the evil-doers. No god of theirs had come to destroy sin and to *save* the sinner as the Lord Jesus had. How she longed that they should have the joy of knowing Him, the God who could deliver them from all their fears as well as from all their sins.

7

A JOY FOR AMY

ONE day Amy and her Indian fellow-workers joined with Mr. Walker and his band of young men for an open-air service at the side of a village well. It was evening and the women and girls were coming to the well to draw water. Among them came a ten-year-old girl named Star.

In the last few months Star had been puzzling over some big problems. She had a very quick temper. When she was playing with other children in the village and something annoying happened, her temper would flare up and before she knew what was happening, she would be shouting angrily at them. Then they would get angry too and refuse to play with her. She tried hard to control her temper and to keep back the sharp words, but she could not do it. She so wanted the other children to like her and to want to play with her that she asked her father which of the gods was the God of gods. She thought that surely the most powerful of all the gods must be able to change dispositions and give her a good temper. Her

46

father had not seemed to know of a god who could do this.

Then there was the question of her little brother. He was the most beautiful fat chuckling little baby in the whole village and she loved him dearly, but when he was nine months old he became ill and died. All the brightness had gone out of the world for her on that sad day, and she had wondered ever since, where had he gone? No one seemed able to give any answer to this question.

*   *   *

Now she stood by the well with her brass water-vessel in her hand, watching the crowd gathered there. There was a talking noise and a singing noise and a box that made a noise, she noticed. (She had never seen a baby organ before, and the sounds that came out of it seemed strange to her.) The talking did not interest her much at first, she was too busy looking at the three white people. One of them (Amy) was wearing a *seelai*, and Star fell in love with her at once.

It was getting late and Star, afraid of lingering in case her mother should punish her, moved to go away. Just then a madman came along and began to make a disturbance. "See the white man beat the madman," shouted the crowd with enthusiasm. This sounded exciting so Star turned back again. The white man very gently led the

47

madman out of the crowd—which was disappointingly dull! At the same moment the Tamil man who was preaching said, "There is a living God. There is a living God. He turned me, a lion, into a lamb." These words gripped her attention.

There is a living God who can change dispositions. This was exactly what Star wanted to know. She ran off home and made up her mind that she would go back to the Christians the next day and see if that white lady in a *seelai* could tell her more.

Accordingly, the next day, she followed the Christian band when they came to her village and she went to their meeting in the evening. Everything she heard was new and strange to her and all she really understood was that the living God hears and answers when people pray to Him. She made up her mind to test this to see if it was true or not. She would pray three prayers to Him and if twice out of the three times He did what she asked, she would know that He really was alive and that He really answered prayer. Star ran towards home. It was getting dark and she saw her mother waiting for her on the doorstep with a knotted grass broom in her hand. This meant punishment. As quick as thought Star prayed, "Oh living God, don't let my mother beat me." Her mother caught her by the arm and pulled her into the house. "Chee," she said, "you perverse one. You have been with those low-caste people."

48

Swish, went the broom with a stinging lash. Was this the way the living God answered prayer? Was all that she had heard about Him just words, after all? Star sobbed bitterly as she lay on her mat in the dark that night.

The next day, in spite of her punishment and disappointment, Star went to the children's meeting again. Amy was taking it, and as she talked about the love of the Lord Jesus, Star was tremendously attracted. This must be true, she felt. She was taken completely by surprise when Amy asked, "Has any child here been punished for coming to hear about Jesus Lord?", and she remained silent. The other children were quick to answer for her and tell Amy how Star's mother had beaten her the night before.

"If that should be again," said Amy, "then let the one who is beaten say over and over the Name of Jesus Lord, looking up to Him inwardly, and He will give patience to endure, and He will give peace and comfort."

Star drank in Amy's words and as she trotted along the road to her home she kept saying, "*Yesu Swami*" [Jesus Lord] to herself lest she should forget. On the way she stopped under a tamarind tree. The fruit hung temptingly ripe. She must not pick it, for that would be stealing, but if it fell by itself she might pick it up and eat it. She prayed, "O Jesus Lord, living God, make the

D

fruit fall." A pod fell at her feet and she picked it up with a wondering heart. It was getting late and she ran down the street somewhat anxiously. "Living God, Jesus Lord, deign to listen; do not let my mother punish me," she prayed. Her mother was waiting. "Come in, child. I thought thou wast lost," she said and ladled some rice into a bowl calling her to supper. There was no punishment.

The question was settled. Jesus Lord was the living God.

*   *   *

Amy had learnt a lot about prayer from her own experience. When she was a child and had prayed for blue eyes God had said, "No." Later when she had asked Him for £500, He had said, "Yes." At Broughton Grange when He had told her to go overseas and she had asked Him where and how, He had first said, "Wait." Many, many other times God had answered her prayers and spoken to her, and now she wanted the children to have the same wonderful experience and so in one of the meetings she talked to them about it.

"He will always listen and always understand," she said, "even if we do not for a little while hear Him answer us, we must not be discouraged; the ear of our soul has to learn to hear. If He does not say *Yes* to something we are asking, but *Wait* or

50

No, we must not be impatient or unhappy as though it meant He did not care. The one sure thing is that He hears and cares. If we listen carefully, sooner or later we shall hear Him speaking softly and very comfortingly to our hearts." Star knew that when her beloved white-lady-who-wears-a-*seelai* spoke like this she was speaking the absolute truth, so from then on she talked to "Jesus Lord" everywhere she went.

Star's family noticed a difference in her. They thought the Christians had bewitched her. Nothing they said and no amount of punishment made any difference, so they decided to send her away to live with an uncle for a little while, and they hoped that there she would forget all the nonsense she had learned from those "low-caste Christians".

In the village to which Star was sent, there were a number of people who called themselves Christians. Star watched them carefully. They did not seem to love the Lord Jesus very much, and their dispositions were not any better than other people's. She was very disappointed and began to lose some of her desire to learn about and to follow Him. Her father, who was very clever, had hoped that exactly this would happen.

If the Lord Jesus had not been the living God she would doubtless soon have forgotten Him, but He had not only answered her prayers, He had also heard and was answering Amy's earnest prayers for the children who had come to her meetings. He had not forgotten Star.

One day an older girl told her that the white-lady-who-wears-a-*seelai* would be in the next village on the following day. Star was thrilled and she made up her mind to go over on Sunday morning to the "temple of the Christians" when they would be worshipping Jesus Lord, and she would see the white-lady-who-wears-a-*seelai* there and hear more about Him from her.

On Sunday morning Amy went to the village church as usual and sat on the floor where she always sat beside a pillar. Presently she noticed a little stranger whom she did not recognize, kneeling just in front of her. She did not know that the small girl was even then speaking to God of her longing to hear of Him and to become a Christian, but she somehow wanted to have the child beside her. One of the other children in church, seeing the expression on Amy's face as she looked at Star, whispered something to her. In a moment she moved to sit beside Amy, blissfully content.

After this Star was a regular visitor at the mission bungalow, and how Amy loved teaching her and talking to her about the Lord Jesus of whom she was so eager to learn. One evening they walked outside into the still brightness of the tropical moonlight and Star plucked up her courage to ask her second big question. "Where do little babies go when they die?" Amy did not know anything about the precious little brother who had died, but she did know the Lord Jesus who is the Lover of children. So she talked to Star about the Good Shepherd who gathers the lambs in His arms and carries them to Love's own Country.

* * *

Amy knew that Star's relatives might forbid her to come to the mission bungalow at any time, and she was anxious to be sure that Star not only knew about the Lord Jesus in her head, but that she had really received Him into her heart to be her Saviour for always. Accordingly, one day, she read to her the nineteenth chapter of St. John's Gospel.

They were on their knees as they read that terrible story of the suffering and death of our Lord Jesus, and He Himself came near and made it very real to Star. As Amy came to the words "They crucified Him" Star could bear it no longer. She covered her face, which was wet with tears, with her hands. "Is it all over?" she sobbed. "Will they ever hurt Him again?" She sighed with relief when Amy told her, "They will never hurt Him again."

Gently Amy explained to Star something of the reason for all that suffering, for "He was

wounded for our transgressions, He was bruised
for our iniquities". Star had wanted to find a God
who could change dispositions, but she had had
no idea that it could possibly cost Him so much
to do it. How wonderful was His love! She sobbed
again as she thought of her own sinfulness and of
His suffering for her, but Amy began to read
other words that He had spoken, "If any man will
open the door I will come in," and Star understood
that He, the living God, was willing to come and
live in her heart, to change her disposition and be
her very own Saviour for always. Then and there
she asked Him to do all this.

Star had many very great difficulties in the
years that followed, but how glad she always was
that the Lord Jesus had made her heart His home.
He never left her and He never disappointed her.

8

THE ELF

FOR several years after Amy joined Mr. and Mrs. Walker, she continued to travel a great deal with her women's evangelistic band, through the villages of the Tirunelveli District. She did not travel vast distances but journeying by bullock-cart or on foot was a long hot tedious business. The district is bounded on the west by the mountains and on the east by the sea. Some of the country through which she passed was wild and lonely. Robbers sometimes lurked behind boulders or among the scrubby thorn bushes waiting to steal their jewels from unwary women travellers. Occasionally the people of the villages in the foot-hills would tell of the ravages of a tiger among their cattle. In camp it was always necessary to be on the alert for snakes and scorpions which have a way of creeping under bedding-rolls or into sandals and providing a nasty surprise for the careless. Food always had to be carefully guarded from the onslaught of hungry crows and rats, and armies of industrious ants which are always on the war-path.

The work itself was hard and often there was much to discourage and disappoint. Amy knew nothing of ease and luxury in these years, but she was content. She had a staunch band of Indian women colleagues who were her dear friends. (Star eventually became one of their number.) God was with them and from time to time they received from Him what Amy called "over-weights of joy" as they saw Him work in seemingly impossible situations.

*   *   *

One day Amy travelled from Dohnavur, where her headquarters were, to the village in the east of the district where she had been living when Star met her in church. She arrived there late in the evening. The next morning early, while she was sitting on the veranda having her breakfast, an elderly woman appeared, leading by the hand a little girl who was certainly not more than six or seven years old. The small girl was chattering gaily to the woman, but when she saw Amy she ran straight to her and climbed on to her knee announcing as she did so "I am Pearl-eyes. I have run and come and now I am going to stay with you always."

The little girl was so attractive that Amy could not help giving her a welcoming hug and a kiss. Then she turned to the woman, a Christian, whom she knew, and asked, "Who is the child? Where has she come from?"

The woman shrugged her shoulders, turning her hands palms uppermost in a gesture of perplexity, and began her story.

"Yesterday evening it was getting dark as I carried my water from the well to my house. As I passed the church I saw her"—nodding towards the child—"standing all alone. It is not good for a girl-child to be alone on the road so late, so I spoke to her. 'Where are you going and who do you want?' I asked. She said she was looking for the 'Child-catching Ammal'." The woman paused and looked embarrassed. "You know the people call you that?" she asked.

Amy nodded. She could never understand why, ever since Belfast days, children always seemed so attracted to her. She loved them of course, but who would not? Naturally she never tried to allure them away from their houses, but some of the Hindu people felt sure she knew a secret charm which made children want to come to her meetings and become Christians. So they called her the Child-catching Ammal.

"I asked her where she had come from and where her mother was," the woman continued, "and she said she had run away from the servants of the gods in the temple over the river. I did not believe her. How could such a small child escape from *them*? But she kept telling me it was so. It was late and the child was alone and just a little green thing, so I took her home with me." A curious expression passed over the woman's face. She was a good-hearted peasant of low caste. "She would not eat rice in my house. She says she is a high-caste child. She went to bed hungry because she would not break the rules of her caste." Her tone was half-admiring and half-angry at the behaviour of her strong-willed little guest.

"Well, it is good that you are here now. I should have taken her back to the temple this morning if you hadn't come. I shouldn't have dared keep her," she said, preparing to leave.

Amy looked at Pearl-eyes and wondered what her story could be. She had given her a doll to play with during her conversation with the village woman, and now she was deeply absorbed in a game.

As she played Amy talked to her. Yes, it was true that she had run away from the temple yesterday. Nobody had seen her go. She had crossed some fields and waded over the river and when she had arrived at the big church it was getting dark. She had stood still and was wondering what to do next when the woman had spoken to her and taken her home.

"I have run and come, and now I will stay with

you," she said with decision. "The servants of the gods don't love me. Nobody loves me. I won't ever go back."

Little by little she told Amy more. Her father had died when she was a baby and she had never known him. When she was very small her mother had taken her to the temple to visit the servants of the gods and had left her with them. She had not been happy. They did not love her as her mother had done. Once, when she had been naughty, they had punished her by burning the backs of her hands with a red-hot iron. So she ran away. She knew that her mother lived in a town twenty miles away and she set out to walk there. She was only six and the roads were long and hot and dusty, but she met kind people who let her walk with them. The journey took three days and how tired she was at the end of it!

When she found her mother, she flung herself into her arms sure that now she would be safe and happy. The temple women had, however, followed her. They talked about the wrath of the gods and her mother listened and was terribly afraid.

"I put my arms round her neck and held on tight," said Pearl-eyes. "But she dragged my arms away and gave me back to the servants of the gods who took me away with them." The little girl's eyes grew big with fear. "I heard them talking. They said they would tie me to the god. I went to look. The god is made of stone and so black and it is dark and lonely in that shrine." She covered her face and shuddered. "So I have run and come. Don't send me back," she pleaded.

*   *   *

Amy took Pearl-eyes to Mr. Walker, who, after questioning her, sent for the Tamil pastor. They sent a messenger to the village from which she said she had come, to find out if her story was true. After a while the messenger returned and said it was quite true that a little girl had run away from the temple women the night before. Almost at once the women themselves arrived looking for the child.

"Who are you and what do you want?" asked Mr. Walker.

"Oh, we are the servants of the gods," said one of them, but another whispered hurriedly to her, "Why do you tell them that?"

They called Pearl-eyes and tried to persuade her to go with them. Amy said nothing, but she did not force the child to go and Pearl-eyes was quite determined to stay with her. After a while the women went away.

Pearl-eyes was shaken. She turned to Amy in distress. "If they come again, please hide me," she begged.

After about an hour a big crowd collected round the veranda and among them was a loud-voiced, hard-faced woman of whom Pearl-eyes seemed to be absolutely terrified.

"If you want to stay here you must say so, out loud, so that everyone can hear," shouted the woman glaring angrily at the child. Pearl-eyes stood trembling. She shrank away from the woman, but not a single word would come.

Someone shouted at the little girl, "You are a dirty thief. We shall get the police to come and take you to prison." Amy and the Walkers asked what she had stolen, and after some time were told four and a half annas (about $4\frac{1}{2}$d.)! Amy paid this sum straight away in front of everybody.

Star had been watching all that was going on and now she came forward and carried off the frightened little girl. She remembered what it felt like to be the centre of shouting and anger and to have everyone's eyes fixed on one, and she knew just how to comfort Pearl-eyes and give her the courage she needed.

Presently they came back to the veranda together and faced the noisy crowd. To the often repeated command to return to the temple Pearl-eyes cried loudly, "I won't! I won't!"

The crowd gradually dispersed, muttering threats about writing to the child's mother. Greatly to the surprise of Amy and the Walkers no letter was ever received and no one ever came back to inquire about Pearl-eyes again. From that day she became Amy's little girl and was nicknamed the Elf.

The Elf regarded Amy as her mother, and so, of course, always called her Amma, which is the Tamil for mother. As time went on so many people called Amy Amma* that it is difficult to think of her by any other name, for the Elf was the first child in what grew to be a very large family indeed.

*   *   *

The Elf told Amma a great many things about her life in the temple, and Amma found out other things from other people. When she spoke of being "tied to the god", the Elf had pictured herself tied with cords to the idol in the dark eerie inner sanctuary of the temple. In Tamil the verb "to tie" can also mean "to marry". Amma understood that the temple women had meant to have a ceremony performed by which the Elf would have been "married" to the god, and so bound to serve that particular god in a particular way for the rest of her life. This would have meant that as she grew older she would have been trained to a life of sin and wickedness from which

* The Tamil word *Amma* is not pronounced quite as it looks. The "A" in the first syllable rhymes with the "u" in up. The second syllable, *ma*, rhymes with Ah!

she could not have escaped. Her mother thought she was pleasing the gods by giving her little daughter to them and that they would regard her family with favour because of the gift.

Many other people in India, at that time, thought that they could win the blessing of the gods in this way and Amma found that very many babies and little girls were given or sold to the temple women in order to be "married" to the gods later. She and her friends quietly investigated this buying and selling of children. As she learnt more she felt increasingly sure that God was calling her to give the rest of her life to rescuing these children and bringing them up for Him.

It was not so very many years since a campaign had been waged in England by the Salvation Army and other social reformers against what was called the white slave traffic, there. This traffic, or trade, concerned the obtaining and selling of little girls by unscrupulous people wholly for the sake of making money. It had been a hard war for the reformers to win, but at last laws were passed forbidding it.

The custom of buying and selling children in India had some connection with religion and so was even harder to stop. Since India became independent in 1947 her government has passed various good laws forbidding this terrible trading of children in connection with the temples, but

Amma's work for the children began in 1901, and at that time there were few who cared for reform of this kind.

Even now there are children in India who need a home and protection from dangers of different kinds, so there is still a Family in Dohnavur, although their Amma has gone to be with the Lord she loved so much.

9

THE FOUNDING OF A FAMILY

AMMA had not realized just at first what a difference the Elf's coming was to make in her life. It was lovely when she arrived home after a long day's work, to find an eager little person waiting to give her an enthusiastic welcome. Amma's tiredness would be all forgotten as she listened to her summary of her day's doings before her goodnight prayers. The account was strictly honest even though the Elf wanted to put herself in the best possible light, and was generally something like this:

"Once I was cross with the Imp," she would begin (the Imp was nine and a half to the Elf's seven and a half and was a playmate). "I was cross because she did not do as I told her. That was wrong of me, but it was wrong of her too, so it was only half a sin. Then I did not do my work well. That was quite all my fault. Then I caught a quarrel with those naughty little children. They were stupid little children and they would not play my game. But they came running after me and they said, 'Please forgive us,' so I forgave

65   E

them. That was very good of me, and I also forgave the Imp so that is three bad things and two good things today."

Here Amma hastily tried to give the Elf a lesson on the evils of pride, but her news was not all told yet and she hurried on with it. Mrs. Walker had given her a piece of soap for her very own, and she had found some "lovely rags" in the waste-paper basket. She had also been given some deliciously sticky cakes which she had hidden in her box among her clothes, for safety.

One day she hit on a wonderful plan for avoiding punishment at school. "I found this cane myself," she announced to her friends, brandishing it cheerfully. "It was lying on the ground in the compound and I am going to take it to the teacher." The other children were astonished. "Why?" they shouted in chorus with evident and apprehensive disapproval. "Because," said the Elf with modest pride in her own cleverness, "if I give it to him with my own hands, how will he cane my hands with it? His heart will not be hard enough to cane me with the cane I gave him!"

*　　*　　*

Amma loved her small Elf more and more with every day that passed. Although it was a constant joy to see her carefree happiness and to listen to her comic chatter, the memory of things she had talked about when she first arrived always haunted Amma. She prayed continually for the other little children who she knew were in danger or perhaps suffering even as the Elf had suffered. God heard her prayers and wonderfully directed and helped her as she tried to find ways of saving children. Before long little ones began to arrive. Some of them were tiny babies needing constant careful attention, but Amma received them gladly. She and her few faithful Indian colleagues soon became so busy caring for babies and toddlers that they had no time for travelling round the district and doing evangelistic work.

Many people, particularly other missionaries, simply could not understand Amma. "You are just a nurse-maid, now," they said, "not a real missionary at all. How can it be right for you to stop teaching the village women about the Lord Jesus, and to spend all your time giving bottles to babies?"

This criticism was hard to bear because it was just what Amma herself was tempted to wonder. She was puzzled and troubled. The work she had been doing before seemed so much bigger and more important than all the dozens of little dull jobs that now filled her days. Was she wasting time?

God kindly answered this question for her by reminding her that His own Son had done the work of a servant when He had washed His disciples' feet. That work had not been a waste of time. God does not waste His servants' time when they are obeying Him. So she continued steadfastly in the new task He had given her and as she did it she began to understand something of His purposes. If He enabled her to bring up her children to be good soldiers of Jesus Christ, they would be able to do far more for Him in their beloved India than she, a foreigner, could ever do. She put some of this thought into verse which is still sung as a prayer for the boys and girls in Dohnavur:

> "Make them valiant warriors, Jesus,
>   Over self and sin;
> Lead them, lead them on to triumph
>   Over foes within.
> Lead them forth in any service
>   Thou, dear Lord, shalt choose,
> Make them steadfast, make them faithful,
>   Meet for Thee to use."

Most mothers would not expect more than, at most, seven or eight babies to be added to their families in ten years. Amma had about two hundred added to hers in that time. No wonder she was busy!

She had never had the kind of training most people feel necessary before undertaking to look after a lot of delicate babies and to bring up and educate numbers of healthy children, so she sometimes made mistakes. Very often things were difficult and she had some big disappointments and sorrows. Some of her precious babies became ill with illnesses she did not understand and in spite of all her loving care some of them died. (The nearest doctor lived more than a day's journey away.) Some of the Christian women who came to help, and whom Amma had expected to become real comrades in the work, found the life too hard and the standards too high and went away again. Nevertheless, through all the stormy beginnings God was with her, teaching her, leading her, and wonderfully providing for all the needs of the ever-growing family.

* * *

Amma sometimes had big worries, but she never let these shadow her children. To them she was the most understanding and loving of mothers, and their life was a carefree and happy one.

She encouraged them to take an interest in the abounding wild life around them. The children enthusiastically rescued baby squirrels that, having fallen from their nests, were in imminent danger of inadvertently providing a succulent meal for raiding crows. These squirrels make engaging pets and can be carried in a pocket or the folds of a *seelai*, from which they regard the world with bright little eyes and inquiringly twitching noses and whiskers. Baby mynas are sometimes dropped by birds of prey startled in flight. These can be taught to talk (they are related to our starlings) and are a never-ending source of interest. A myna called Jim was a very special favourite and a fluent conversationalist. He was once found standing in front of Kŭt the cat and asking considerately, "Are you hungry?" Fortunately Kŭt was a well-mannered cat and refrained from making a meal of Jim. Once an excited deputation of children rushed to Amma calling her to come and see a marvellous snake that "stands up and makes an arch". She arrived to find an admiring circle of children around a cobra with its hood spread and its head raised ready to strike. Its bite would have meant death for any child. How grateful Amma was to the guardian angels who, it seemed, so often protected her children from harm.

Amma very well understood the fascinating attraction that the topmost branches of the big old tamarind tree in the garden had for the venturesome children. There was one child who would climb until her head and shoulders stuck out from the greenery at the very top of the tree. There she would stand joyfully surveying the scene and singing at the top of her voice. Amma did have some bad moments when a tiny child was found walking precariously on the narrow wall surrounding a deep well, but she was glad when the children were fearless. She taught them to swim while they were very young, and they had wonderful games in the big irrigation wells, some of which are the size of a small swimming-bath, but with no shallow end.

In such a big family it was very necessary for everyone, even very small people, to take some share in household chores. Fortunately in country districts of South India life is simple. People like to eat rice for breakfast, dinner and supper. It may be cooked in various ways and is eaten with a great variety of different curries or chutney or pickles and is never at all like the rice pudding abhorred of many at school dinners in England. It is eaten with the fingers of the right hand, from a brass bowl. Washing up is simple and very quick. Each child washes her fingers, her mouth and her own rice-bowl, and that is all there is to it.

There is not much furniture in most South Indian houses and the majority of people sleep on grass mats on the floor with, perhaps, a cotton sheet for covering if the weather is cool. In the morning the sheet is folded and the mat rolled up and stacked neatly and that is the end of bed-making. The part of the house demanding most attention is the floor on which you sit to eat and work, and on which you lie to sleep. In Dohnavur the red floor-tiles are swept and washed until they shine, and guests ask what polish is used on them. (The answer of course is elbow-grease.) The paths around the houses also need to be swept clean, for rubbish around a house is a disgrace to the owner. Plants and flowers, which are a constant joy to the family, demand much watering in a country where weeks pass without a drop of rain. Water is not laid on through pipes, so this involves much carrying of buckets from wells or pumps, but it is a labour of love and worth the trouble.

Some children in the early days and in every generation since have found housework very boring and the discipline that goes with it hard to bear. Amma wrote a song to help them. It goes with a swing to a jolly tune:

> "Hate not laborious work,
>   Joy, joy is in it;
>   Do not thy duty shirk,
>   Joy, joy is in it;
>   Welcome the daily round,
>   On, and be faithful found,
>   On, and thou shalt be crowned,
>   Joy, joy is in it."

Amma wanted her children above all things to be faithful and absolutely trustworthy. That was one of the reasons why her sharp eyes were so observant about the dark corners in the backs of their rooms which most people might not notice. It was tempting to scamp dusting the backs of things and to bundle untidy oddments in a messy jumble behind a locker where they *might* not be noticed, but Amma wanted the children to be faithful in these little things remembering that the Lord Jesus sees and knows even when no one else does.

*   *   *

As time went on Amma prayed very definitely for more helpers. God sent her a nurse from England, and then at intervals three trained teachers. They came at a time when some of the first children were growing up and needing more serious education than Amma had had time to give. Later more workers were given and the Dohnavur Fellowship came into being. Always there was more work to do than could be satisfactorily accomplished by the small number of people there to do it. Is it possible that some whom God would have liked to send said "no" to Him? To say "no" to God always brings terrible loss.

It took some time for the teachers from overseas to learn how to handle their new pupils, who could not always resist the temptation to play up and see just how far they could go with them. One day Chellalu, a ringleader in all mischief, had been more than usually full of bright ideas and at last the harassed Sittie (as the workers from overseas were called) wrote a note and gave it to her, telling her to take it to Amma.

Chellalu sobered at once. Sittie would only write a note to describe crimes that were very bad indeed. What would Amma say, and still worse, what would she do when she read it? Chellalu considered. It would not do to throw the note away. She must go with it to Amma. Suddenly she saw the solution.

"Amma, Chellalu," she called on Amma's doorstep.

"Come Chellalu," said Amma. Then with some anxiety she added, "Why aren't you in school?"

"Sittie sent me to you with a note," said Chellalu demurely dropping her eyes which glinted wickedly.

"Well, where is the note?" inquired Amma sternly.

"Amma, I've eaten it!" announced the incorrigible Chellalu.

10

LOTUS BUDS AND THE GREY FOREST

WHILE Amma's family was still fairly small and the majority of the children were quite young, she wrote a book. She had written several others earlier, but this book was full of photographs of small children and babies and contained many stories about them too. Amma called the book *Lotus Buds*, and ever since it was published in 1909 people in many parts of the world have thought of the small girls of the Dohnavur Family as Lotus Buds.

It is a nice name. This particular kind of water-lily is symbolic, in India, of all that is pure and beautiful. The name gives the Lotus Buds a very high standard at which to aim, but there is one respect in which it is not really very appropriate. Lotus lilies are so still and quiet, and that could certainly never be said of the Dohnavur Buds!

As the years went by Amma and her Indian and European helpers often felt very, very tired. The weather in Dohnavur is, roughly speaking, hot, hotter and hottest. It is lovely never to be cold, but it is also rather tiring always to be hot—

and busy as well. It seemed essential that they should all get away to a cooler place for a rest now and then, but how could they leave the Lotus Buds? The hill resorts to which Europeans usually go for holidays can only be reached by a long, tedious, expensive, railway journey. Nowhere in these places would there be accommodation for dozens of assorted children as well as for the adults.

Amma looked longingly at the green forest-clad mountains just behind Dohnavur. Would it be possible to buy a slice of mountain and build a holiday home there, she wondered? She began to pray about the possibility and also to prospect. There were no motor roads up the mountains and of course no railways. The only way to explore them was to walk up the steep forest tracks, or to travel in a mountain-chair carried on the shoulders of men. Amma often had to submit to the latter method although she would much have preferred to walk. More than twenty years in the tropics had deprived her of much of her physical strength, but had not made a scrap of difference to her spirit or courage. At last, after many fruitless journeys, she found an ideal spot. It was a disused coffee-garden of about forty acres in a valley nine miles or so from Dohnavur. It was between 2,500 and 3,000 feet above sea level and ever so much cooler than the burning plains. It belonged to a

Muslim man and the price he asked for it was £100.

*   *   *

A hundred pounds! It was a large sum to pay for land in a relatively inaccessible spot. Amma knew that there would also be the big expense of building and of carrying necessary materials up the mountain. Was it right to buy?

Amma asked God to show her what He wanted her to do. She was very anxious not to waste any of the money He had given or to buy something which might prove to be an embarrassing expense in the future. She asked God to give her a sign. If He wanted her to buy, she asked that He would send her £100 all in one gift. She very seldom received so much money in a single amount, so such a gift would be a clear sign.

God understood His servant's doubts and fears and so in His kindness (and this is just the kind of thing God loves to do for His children) He sent her three separate gifts of exactly £100. Now, with a thrice repeated sign, all her doubts disappeared, and very joyfully she bought the land.

There followed a time of strenuous adventure for Amma and the Lotus Buds. They went to the Grey Forest (for that is its very inappropriate name) and camped there to superintend and help in the building of their house. The workmen who came up from the plains did not like the place. When it rained they found it bitterly cold and they wanted to return to the warmth of their villages. There had been a demon shrine on the site and they were terribly afraid that he (the demon) would be angry with them for demolishing the shrine and in revenge would cause disaster of some kind.

The Lotus Buds worked in a most un-bud-like way, carrying up the steep slope from the river loads of sand and stone that were needed for the building. Time and again lazy or frightened work-men were shamed into continuing work by Amma's imperturbable cheerfulness and the hard steady work of the girls.

There were some narrow escapes and near-catastrophes during building operations, but the men could not help being impressed by the way God answered prayer and made seemingly impossible things possible. Night after night they gathered round to listen as Amma led an informal meeting for them. Eventually two of them asked the Lord Jesus to come into their hearts and then bravely confessed their faith in Him in front of their fellow-workmen.

The fun of the Forest really began in those days of hard work with Amma, and it has not been exhausted yet.

* * *

The Forest House, as that first house was called (for other houses were built later) is encircled by mountains on three sides. To the east the forest falls steeply away to the shimmering red plains and the distant blue sea. Through the rocky ravine tumbles a clear river that never quite dries up in drought and that roars down the mountain in a series of impressive cascades when it is in spate. Near the Forest House a deep pool glints cool and green. Its Tamil name is the Emerald Pool and in it enthusiasts can swim and dive and perform endless aquatic feats to their hearts' content.

Our Forest is a naturalists' paradise with numerous species of gay birds; countless kinds of butterflies, moths and insects of all varieties; and many rare and interesting wild flowers including orchids. Elephants, tigers, panthers, bears, red dogs, various kinds of deer, mountain goats, three different kinds of monkey and many other wild animals have all been seen at different times by members of the Family. The possibility of a bear on a quiet path is a strong temptation to hardy practical jokers. Amma herself was a past master at realistic bear grunts guaranteed to send the timid scurrying for help!

The mountains invite exploration and in the course of the years the older brothers of the Family have cut paths through the forest to the summits. Long hikes, and picnics, of the proper kind involving a camp fire and the brewing of coffee, are part of the habitual joys of the Family's holidays now.

11

MORE ANSWERED PRAYER

IT WAS a good thing that Amma had had much experience and practice in praying before she became responsible for a large family of children. There was no one in the whole world who had undertaken to support them. Year by year the Family grew bigger, and year by year expenses grew bigger too.

Prayer is a very simple thing, but the kind of prayer that God hears and answers is never really easy. There are conditions to be fulfilled. Sometimes when supplies of money and of food got very low and it seemed that her prayers were unanswered Amma would search her own heart in deep distress to see if perhaps she had failed to fulfil the conditions. Did God see in her some disobedience, some unbelief, some failure to put Him first, that made it impossible for Him to answer her prayers for the children's needs, she wondered? She was absolutely dependent on Him for everything. Constantly she carefully studied His word in order that she might know Him better and also know His will for her and the Family.

One day when the Family was still quite small, Amma found that they were at the end of their store of rice. A merchant arrived at the bungalow with rice to sell at a reasonable price, but Amma had no money with which to buy. Could it be that the children would have to go hungry? Such a thing had never happened. Amma called the Family together and explained the situation. Then they all knelt in a big circle and told God of their difficulty and need.

None of them noticed a little playmate from the village who was watching with round-eyed interest.

Even as they prayed they were interrupted by the arrival of a messenger from Tirunelveli. He handed an envelope to Amma. She opened it and out dropped one hundred rupees! The prayer meeting was turned to a praise meeting, and rice sufficient for their needs was bought at once.

To the little Hindu village girl who was watching, it could hardly have seemed more wonderful if the skies had opened and a hundred rupees had dropped straight from Heaven. What a powerful God these Christians worshipped! Deeply impressed she trotted off home.

*   *   *

The years passed and God continued to provide money as it was needed, not only for food, but also for buildings. Many new houses were built and also schools and a church, which is called the House of Prayer and which stands in the centre of the Compound. In 1918 little boys as well as little girls began to join the Family and later men as well as women workers were given. With stalwart brothers to run it, a farm, with rice land and a dairy herd and fruit gardens, was gradually built up and established.

Now it was no longer necessary to buy rice, but the Family was still as directly dependent as ever upon God for the supply of their daily food.

One year there was good rain at the beginning of the wet season towards the end of October and the seed-beds were sown. The seedlings were progressing nicely when the weather turned un-seasonably hot and dry for a few days. This was long enough for myriads of caterpillars to hatch out in the hot sun. There were so many that it looked as if all the seedlings would be completely eaten up in a matter of a few days. The man in charge of the rice-land saw the danger to the crop and went home and told Amma and the Family and asked them all to pray for God's protection. Even small five- and six-year-old children under-stood about the caterpillars and prayed.

Two days later when he went to look at the

fields again, he saw a very unexpected sight. Marching up and down the lines of seedlings were lots of cattle egrets (white birds rather like herons) greedily feasting on the caterpillars. A day or two later there was not a caterpillar left, and the seedlings were undamaged.

Other people's seedlings in much of the surrounding countryside were completely destroyed by the caterpillars. It is the custom of the Dohnavur Family to pray, not only for the crops belonging to themselves, but also for those on all the surrounding land. On this occasion and some few others, God saw fit to protect only the seedlings belonging to those people who openly acknowledged Him as Lord. The people in the villages near at hand had all heard of Him and could have prayed to Him too, but most of them were continuing to call upon other gods for help. These gods failed to hear or to give protection. Our God showed Himself to be the Living God, who answers prayer.

*   *   *

A year or two after the egrets saved the rice crop, the Dohnavur Family found itself in another quite different kind of difficulty.

A man who, with his family, had received a lot of help from Amma became discontented and fancied he had a grievance. He had received much but he wanted more. When he found that Amma and those helping her did not intend to do exactly as he asked he was very angry. He began stirring up bitter feeling against the Family among the village folk. He fixed up a loudspeaker on the wall of the Compound and for a whole night shouted torrents of abuse through it. No one could sleep that night and it was a severe trial for Amma, who was ill, to have to listen to all the false and venomous accusations of this man she had truly wanted to help.

He still felt his revenge was incomplete, and word came from a reliable source to say that he had hired a gang of young toughs to come and break down the Compound gates. This was serious. The Fellowship members met that evening to pray for God's protection for the Compound and all the children. Amma, in bed in the next room, was praying too and able to hear enough of what was going on to follow the trend of the prayer meeting. Those gathered together had intended to go on praying all night, if necessary, but after a short time everyone present was quite convinced that God had already heard and answered their prayer. There was nothing further to do except to say "thank you" and go to bed and to sleep.

The gangsters did not come that night. Days and weeks went by and everything remained peaceful.

Then one day a Fellowship member waiting for a bus overheard an interesting conversation between two village women.

"I was in my house one evening," said one woman to the other, "when I heard a talking noise in the next house. It was a crowd of wild young men. They were talking about going to Dohnavur and breaking down the gates. I listened to their talk and I was afraid. At last I went to them. After all I am old and sometimes the young respect grey hairs. I said to them, 'You had better be very careful what you do. Those people at Dohnavur worship a very powerful God. I once saw the Amma pray for money when she needed to buy rice for the children. *At once* her God heard, and He sent her a hundred rupees. I saw it with my own eyes. He is very powerful and you had better be careful. Those people at Dohnavur may not send for the police, but they will pray to their God.' Those wild young men were silent when they heard me speak, for they were afraid. When I left them they went away."

It says in the Bible that God is able to do exceedingly abundantly above all that we ask or think. Who would have thought that in answer to prayer for money for rice, God would not only give more than was needed at the time, but would also give protection from gangsters many years later?

Amma constantly prayed that her children might grow up to be steadfast and faithful and used by the Lord Jesus in His service. She lived to see this prayer answered in very many ways.

Some have taken on the care of babies or older children or have become teachers in the schools. Others have worked steadily at jobs which may not sound so interesting, but are absolutely essential for the welfare of the Family. The work of rescuing and making a home for the children in danger could never have continued but for the loving service of many of the grown-up boys and girls of the Family. Still others are doing good work in other parts of India.

It is sad to have to write that there are some for whom this prayer has not yet been answered. There are some who want to run their own lives and although they want to receive good things from Him, they do not want to give the Lord Jesus anything costly. Faithful, steadfast service is always costly, of course.

Amma continued to pray for her dear Family right to the end of her life. The story of the answers to these prayers cannot be completed yet, for God is still working.

*　　*　　*

When Amma began to work for the children she found it very difficult to give up her work in the villages, and although she was comforted by remembering that the Lord Jesus Himself did the work of a servant, she never forgot the people outside the Compound and always longed to be able to help them more. God gave her an assurance that since she could not go to them, He would bring needy people to her. Again and again He did this. Sometimes it was very poor humble folk who came. At other times it was important people like Government officials whom no one would have suspected of being in need.

Once a high-caste widow woman arrived. Life for her had been very sad since the death of her husband. Everyone told her, and she fully believed, that some sin of hers had, like a poisonous snake, bitten and destroyed her husband's life. So she was despised and everyone thought of her as a bringer of bad luck. No one sympathized with her loneliness and sorrow. At last, after years of miserable solitude, she went on a pilgrimage. She visited all the holy places of South India looking for peace and forgiveness of sins. At each temple and shrine she was told to give alms and so she spent much money, but she did not find peace and her sin remained as a heavy burden. At last she chanced to come to Dohnavur. There to her immense surprise she heard from Amma and others of a God whose first word to those who want to worship Him is not "Give" but "Take".

With joy she received from Him His gifts of forgiveness and peace and new life. She has been
telling other people about her Saviour Jesus
Christ, ever since.

This kind of experience was tremendously
cheering to Amma, but she still kept thinking of
all the ill people in the villages and particularly of
the women and children who at that time had no
one to help them when they were in pain. In 1921
her prayers for them became very definite and she
and some of her colleagues asked God for a
hospital. It was not to be a formal terrifying kind
of place, but a place where people coming for help
would be loved and made to feel at home and
served for love of the Lord Jesus. Amma prayed
for doctors and nurses to staff it, for instruments
and medicines to equip it, and for money to build it.

God gave all these and much more besides, but
just over fifteen years were to pass from the time
of the first united definite prayer for a hospital to
the time of its opening. All through this long
waiting period God gave signs that He was still
working to answer prayers. ·Doctors and nurses
were given from Britain, Switzerland and
Germany. These quickly got to work even before
the hospital buildings were ready, and not only
helped the village folk but also began the training
of young men and women of the Family for what
was to be.

A gift of £100, specially for a hospital, seemed like God's signal to go ahead with building plans, but when they came to consider the matter in detail, those in Dohnavur realized that to build and equip a hospital would cost about £10,000.

In the early days one hundred rupees (which is about £7) had seemed a large sum of money. Later, when Amma was praying about buying land in the mountains, £100 had seemed a vast amount to ask God to give. Now one of the Fellowship felt God was urging him to ask for £1,000 all in one gift, as a sign that it was right to proceed with such an expensive undertaking. Just as the Family was celebrating Amma's birthday feast in 1929 a cablegram arrived for her announcing that a gift of £1,000 was on its way! Before the buildings were complete, God gave a further sign of His approval by sending another gift of £1,000. The rest of the £10,000 was made up of many small presents, some of them pennies sent by children from different parts of the world. No one was *asked* to give and only God had been told of the amount of money needed, but all was given.

When the hospital was opened in 1936 and work was begun there, by far the greater number of the staff were men and women who had grown up in the Dohnavur Family. Amma herself could not relieve the suffering of the village folk or tell them of the Lord Jesus, but now her children had abundant opportunities for doing this work, opportunities which have increased with each passing year.

12

END OF THE STORY

WHEN Amma first settled in India one of the nicknames which was secretly given her was "The Hare". This was because she was so quick in her movements and so anxious not to waste a precious minute. An Indian lady who had worked with her at that time remembered, many years later, that she did not walk or even run, but seemed to fly. "And frequently, yes frequently, she said to me, 'Art thou an elephant to walk so very slowly?'"

It must have been very, very difficult for such an active person to be suddenly turned into a crippled invalid.

Amma had rented a house in a neighbouring town for some of the Family to use as a medical and evangelistic centre. She went over to see that everything had been properly prepared for those who were to move into it. The key of the house could not be found, and when at last it was forthcoming the daylight was almost gone. Amma hurried through the house inspecting everything.

In the backyard she fell into a hole, which she had not noticed in the gathering darkness. Her leg was broken, and in spite of all the help that could be given her by the surgeon of the hospital at Neyyoor and the doctors at Dohnavur, she was never able to walk again without pain. For very nearly twenty years she scarcely left her room, and for the last two and a half years of her life she could not get out of bed at all. She had worked very hard in India for thirty-seven years before the accident happened. Many people would have felt that, after such long service, illness and pain made an adequate excuse for retirement; but not Amma.

*　　*　　*

Her room was a gay and happy place. In part of the veranda was an aviary where cheerful birds chirruped and flew around displaying their bright colours. Often there was a dog on or under her bed. She always had flowers (unless the ones brought to her were specially attractive, when she would probably give them all away), and often some special treasure such as a rare and beautiful shell for the entertainment of her visitors. She had books and books and books, and was always eager to share them with anyone interested. She did much of her own reading at night since she often found sleep difficult.

In the daytime Amma was rarely alone. People came to her for advice on all sorts of problems. They came for help in personal matters and for direction in matters concerning the Family. They also came to share interesting bits of news, to laugh over comic happenings, or to pray over difficulties and sorrows. Everyone was welcome and Amma was always a most interested listener. She hardly ever spoke of herself and hated "a fuss".

People in almost every quarter of the globe wrote to Amma and she spent much of her time answering letters.

In such intervals as were left she wrote a number of books. She had done a lot of writing from the time she went to Japan and all through her years in India. Now, at the end of her life when she was tempted to feel that her work was finished, God used her writing more than ever.

She could not possibly see *all* her Family every day, but most days she wrote them a message that was copied and fixed to the various notice-boards so that all could read it. In this message she told her Family something of what God had said to her early in the morning as she read her Bible and prayed. These notes made her seem very near and helped people not to miss her going and coming among them quite so much.

★　　★　　★

Towards the end of her life Amma became very tired and ill and greatly longed for the time when the Lord would take her to be with Himself. On January 18, 1951, this longing was fulfilled.

Amma would have been glad to see what followed on that day. Perhaps the Lord whom she loved so much allowed her to see and know some of it.

The boys and men carried her to the village church and as they went they sang songs about Heaven. It was hard for the Family to say goodbye to their beloved Amma, but God Himself gave many of them wonderful courage. They continued to sing for the next hour and a half and people came to the church from far and near to look and to listen. Christian people have something to sing and rejoice about at such times, and Hindus are amazed, for they wail and lament hopelessly at funerals. Amma's going to be with the Lord was not the sad end of a useful life of service, it was a glorious new beginning.

For those who love her and who also love and trust her Saviour, although they are separated from her for the present, there is the certainty of a wonderful reunion some day in the fulness of the joy of the Lord's own presence.

After the singing in the village church was over,

the bells of our own House of Prayer pealed out
triumphantly:

> "The strife is o'er, the battle done;
> The victory of life is won;
> The song of triumph has begun.
> Alleluia!"